Nutrition

Jayne Denshire

Smart Apple Media
P.O. Box 3263
Mankato, MN, 56002

First published in 2010 by
MACMILLAN EDUCATION AUSTRALIA PTY LTD
15–19 Claremont St, South Yarra, Australia 3141

Visit our web site at www.macmillan.com.au or go directly to www.macmillanlibrary.com.au

Associated companies and representatives throughout the world.

Copyright © Jayne Denshire 2010

Library of Congress Cataloging-in-Publication Data

Denshire, Jayne.
Nutrition / Jayne Denshire.
       p. cm. — (Healthy habits)
Includes index.
ISBN 978-1-59920-549-6 (library binding)
1. Nutrition—Juvenile literature. I. Title.
QP141.D44 2011
612.3—dc22

                              2009038472

Edited by Helena Newton
Text and cover design by Kerri Wilson
Page layout by Domenic Lauricella
Photo research by Jes Senbergs
Illustrations by Richard Morden

Manufactured in China by Macmillan Production (Asia) Ltd.
Kwun Tong, Kowloon, Hong Kong
Supplier Code: CP December 2009

Acknowledgments
The author and the publisher are grateful to the following for permission to reproduce copyright material:

Front cover photograph: Boy eating lunch courtesy of Jupiter Images

© Jim Craigmyle/Corbis, 9; © Jozsef Balaton/EPA/Corbis, 25 (top); © J. Garcia/Photocuisine/Corbis, 11; © Olivia Baumgartner/ Sygma/Corbis, 7 (middle); Jose Luis Pelaez/Getty Images, 19; Ragnar Schmuck/Getty Images, 24; iStockphoto, 6 (top); © Kim Gunkel/iStockphoto, 7 (bottom); © Drew Hadley/iStockphoto, 25 (bottom); © Jack Jelly/iStockphoto, 20; © Morgan Lane/ iStockphoto, 3 (top left), 13 (top right); © Rich Legg/iStockphoto, 16; © Olga Lupol/iStockphoto, 13 (bottom left); © Juan Monino/ iStockphoto, 7 (top); © Denis Pepin/iStockphoto, 10; © Glenda Powers/iStockphoto, 6 (bottom); © Eva Serrabassa/iStockphoto, 21; © Nikolay Suslov/iStockphoto, 13 (bottom right); © Zone Creative/iStockphoto, 13 (middle); Jupiter Images, 1, 3, 6 (middle), 12, 14, 15, 17, 18, 22; Photolibrary © Imagebroker/Alamy, 5; Photolibrary © Tony Rusecki Lifestyle/Alamy, 23; © Monkey Business Images/Shutterstock, 4, 8; Stockxpert, 26.

While every care has been taken to trace and acknowledge copyright, the publisher tenders their apologies for any accidental infringement where copyright has proved untraceable. Where the attempt has been unsuccessful, the publisher welcomes information that would redress the situation.

Contents

Healthy Habits 4

What Is Nutrition? 8

Where Do Nutrients Come From? 10

A Balanced Diet 12

What to Eat 14

When to Eat 18

Energy from Food 20

Nutritional Problems 22

People Who Help Us with Nutrition 24

Make Nutrition a Healthy Habit 26

Try This Healthy Habit! 28

Amazing Nutrition Facts 30

Glossary 31

Index 32

When a word is printed in **bold**, you can look up its meaning in the Glossary on page 31.

Healthy Habits

Healthy habits are actions we learn and understandings we develop. These actions and understandings help us be happy and healthy human beings.

Getting out in the fresh air is a healthy habit we can all learn.

If we do something often, we can carry out the action without thinking about it. This action is called a habit.

Putting on a hat every time you go out in the sun is a healthy habit.

Developing Healthy Habits

If we develop healthy habits when we are young, they become good choices for life. We can develop healthy habits in these six ways.

1 Exercise
Good exercise habits keep us fit and healthy.

2 Hygiene
Good **hygiene** habits keep us clean and healthy.

3 Nutrition
Good **nutrition** habits keep us growing and healthy.

4 Rest and sleep
Good rest and sleep habits keep us relaxed, energetic, and healthy.

5 Safety
Good safety habits keep us safe and healthy.

6 Well-being
Good **well-being** habits keep us feeling happy and healthy.

What is Nutrition?

Nutrition is what your body takes in and uses from the food you eat. Good nutrition allows your body to grow well and stay healthy.

Eating fresh food is an important part of good nutrition.

Most food contains **nutrients**, which are the healthy parts of food. Eating and **digesting** nutrients gives your body energy to make **body tissue**. Nutrients **nourish** you so that you grow.

The nutrients in food help you to grow taller.

Where Do Nutrients Come From?

Nutrients come from eating healthy food. But not all foods contain the same nutrients. It is important to eat a range of foods for good nutrition.

Eating plenty of fresh fruit and vegetables will give your body important nutrients.

Vitamins and **minerals** are nutrients. They are necessary for a healthy body. They help your body to grow and to fight **infection**.

Vitamin C is found in citrus fruits such as oranges, lemons, and limes.

A Balanced Diet

To have a healthy or balanced diet, you need to eat a variety of foods. Each food belongs to a food group. A healthy diet includes food from each group every day.

A balanced diet includes a variety of foods.

There are five main food groups. Each group contains foods with similar nutrients.

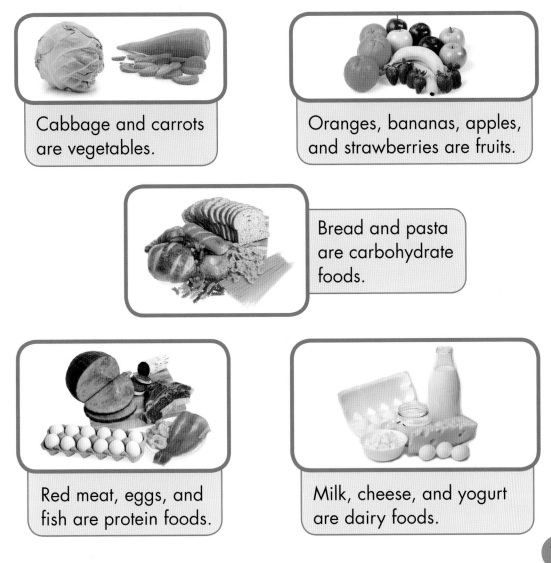

Cabbage and carrots are vegetables.

Oranges, bananas, apples, and strawberries are fruits.

Bread and pasta are carbohydrate foods.

Red meat, eggs, and fish are protein foods.

Milk, cheese, and yogurt are dairy foods.

What to Eat

It is healthy to eat more of some foods and less of others.

"Always Foods"

"Always foods" come from plants and are healthy to eat all the time.

Fruit, vegetables, and bread are "always foods" that have nutrients to help keep you healthy.

"Often Foods"

"Often foods" should be eaten several times a day. Some "often foods" contain protein, which builds up your muscles and helps repair injuries. Dairy foods contain **calcium** for strong bones.

You can eat three servings of dairy foods, such as yogurt and cheese, each day.

"Sometimes Foods"

"Sometimes foods" may taste good but do not have many nutrients. It is better to have these foods occasionally as a treat, rather than every day.

Food such as cake contains sugar and fat, and should only be eaten sometimes.

Water

Drinking plenty of water is an important part of good nutrition. Water helps your body work well and helps your brain think clearly.

Drinking plenty of water each day will help you stay healthy.

When to Eat

It is important to eat regularly for your body to work well. Three balanced meals a day give you the food you need for a healthy body.

Eating regular meals is a good nutrition habit.

Breakfast is the most important meal of the day. It gives you energy to get you and your brain going for the day.

Cereal with milk and freshly squeezed orange juice are healthy breakfast foods.

Energy from Food

The amount of energy in food is measured in calories. The higher the amount of calories, the more energy the food gives your body.

Steak and noodles are high-calorie foods, and vegetables are low-calorie foods.

A Healthy Weight

Your healthy weight depends on your height. The taller you are, the more you should weigh. To keep your weight healthy, you need to use all the calories you take in.

You use up calories from food when you run and play.

Nutritional Problems

Some people have diseases that affect the nutrition in their bodies. Two of these diseases are diabetes and celiac [*say* see-li-ak] disease.

A person with a disease that affects his or her nutrition often gets very tired.

People with diabetes have too much **glucose** in their blood. People with celiac disease cannot eat **gluten**.

People with diabetes use special testers to check how much glucose is in their blood.

People Who Help Us with Nutrition

Some people have jobs in nutrition. Dieticians, food technologists, and chefs all work to help us with nutrition.

Dieticians advise how to eat well for good health. They teach people about good nutrition and can develop special diets for people.

Food technologists develop recipes and determine how to create new food products. They also make sure food is safe to eat.

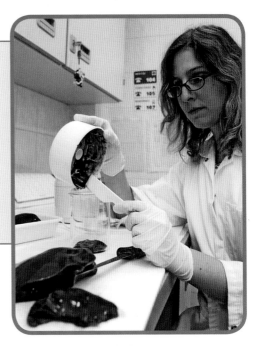

Chefs are trained cooks. They make different types of foods for lots of people.

Make Nutrition a Healthy Habit

Making nutrition a healthy habit means eating a range of healthy foods. Good nutrition habits are important to keep you growing and healthy.

Taking a healthy lunch to school is a good nutrition habit.

Healthy Nutrition Checklist

This checklist shows how often you should do these healthy nutrition habits.

Healthy Nutrition Habit	every day	occasionally, as a treat
eat a balanced diet	✔	
eat sugary food		✔
eat fatty food		✔
drink lots of water	✔	
have a healthy breakfast	✔	
drink sweet, carbonated drinks		✔
be active to use up the calories you have taken in	✔	

Try This Healthy Habit!

You can make a healthy fruit shake for a snack or for breakfast. This makes one drink.

What You Need:

- 8 ounces (250 milliliters) of low-fat milk
- I tablespoon of low-fat plain yogurt
- I teaspoon of honey
- I tablespoon of oat bran
- I serving of fruit, such as one banana or a handful of berries
- a pinch of cinnamon (a spice)
- an electric blender
- a tall glass

You can ask a parent for help.

What To Do:

1   Put the blender on your kitchen counter and plug it in.

2   Place all the ingredients except the cinnamon into the blender.

3   Put the lid on the blender. Make sure it fits tightly.

4   Turn on the blender, slowly at first.

5   Gradually turn up the speed of the blender so that it is at medium speed.

6   Keep blending until a thick, creamy mix forms.

7   Turn off the blender and unplug it.

8   Open the lid of the blender, then pour the mix into a tall glass.

9   Sprinkle a pinch of cinnamon on top.

10   Enjoy your shake!

Amazing Nutrition Facts

Carrots do help you see better! Carrots have **beta carotene**, which is a nutrient that is good for healthier eyesight.

It is the sugar in bread that makes it golden when you toast it.

Fiber helps our digestion. It is found in food such as green vegetables and grainy breads.

Soy milk contains less calcium than cow's milk.

You should drink an extra glass of water for every 45 minutes you exercise.

There are 13 vitamins that your body needs. Eight of these are part of the vitamin B group.

Glossary

beta carotene an essential nutrient found in some orange fruits and vegetables, and leafy green vegetables

body tissue what a living thing is made of

calcium a soft, white metal found in teeth and bones

digesting breaking down food so that it can be absorbed into the body

glucose a natural sugar

gluten a protein found in grains such as rye, wheat, and oats

hygiene what we do to keep ourselves clean and healthy

infection the spread of germs or a disease

minerals substances found in foods that we need to stay healthy, such as calcium, iron, and zinc

nourish to feed healthily

nutrients the healthy parts of food that we need to live and grow

nutrition what our bodies take in and use from the food we eat

vitamins substances found in food that we need to stay healthy, such as Vitamin C

well-being a state of feeling healthy and happy

Index

b
balanced diet   12–13, 18, 27
breakfast   19, 27, 28

c
calcium   15, 30
calories   20–21, 27
carbohydrates   13
celiac disease   22, 23
chefs   24, 25

d
dairy foods   13, 15
diabetes   22, 23
dieticians   24
drinks   17, 27, 28–29, 30

e
energy   19, 20

f
fat   16, 27
food groups   12–13
food technologists   24, 25
fruit   10, 11, 13, 14, 28

g
glucose   23
gluten   23
growth   6, 8, 9, 11, 26

m
minerals   11

n
nutrients   9, 10–11, 13, 14,
    16

p
protein   13, 15

s
sugar   16, 27, 30

v
vegetables   10, 13, 14, 20, 30
vitamins   11, 30

w
water   17, 27, 30
weight   21, 26, 27